CUSTOMER CENTRICITY & GLOBALISATION

Project Management: Manufacturing & IT Services
Kaizen, Agile, Scrum & Managing Global Projects
Ten Commandments Of Customer Centricity

Chandra Sekar

PARTRIDGE

Copyright © 2024 by Chandra Sekar.

ISBN:	Hardcover	978-1-5437-0953-7
	Softcover	978-1-5437-0952-0
	eBook	978-1-5437-0951-3

All rights reserved. No part of this book may be used or reproduced by any means, graphic, electronic, or mechanical, including photocopying, recording, taping or by any information storage retrieval system without the written permission of the author except in the case of brief quotations embodied in critical articles and reviews.

Because of the dynamic nature of the Internet, any web addresses or links contained in this book may have changed since publication and may no longer be valid. The views expressed in this work are solely those of the author and do not necessarily reflect the views of the publisher, and the publisher hereby disclaims any responsibility for them.

Print information available on the last page.

To order additional copies of this book, contact
Partridge India
000 800 919 0634 (Call Free)
+91 000 80091 90634 (Outside India)
orders.india@partridgepublishing.com

www.partridgepublishing.com/india

Contents

Chapter 1   Ten Commandments of Customer Centricity 1
Chapter 2   Metrics and Importance of Competence 4
Chapter 3   Customer Satisfaction Index Measurement 8
Chapter 4   Transforming Customer Satisfaction to Customer Delight 11
Chapter 5   Transforming Customers from Customer Delight to Happy
            Customer 15
Chapter 6   Customer Centricity & Quality Function Deployment 20
Chapter 7   Customer Centricity & Design Thinking 24
Chapter 8   Customer Centricity & Stepping Up Value Chains 27
Chapter 9   Customer Centricity & IT Project Management 29
Chapter 10 Customer Centricity with Agile & Scrum 32
Chapter 11 Azure & Project Management 40
Chapter 12 Customer Centricity & Market Demands 53

CHAPTER I

Ten Commandments of Customer Centricity

#1

CUSTOMERS COME TO us for the relatively lowest price and stay with us for the highest quality.

#2

A happy customer is your free publicity worldwide. There is a clear distinction between Customer satisfaction, customer delight, and Happy customers.

The faster organizations move customers from satisfaction level to Happiness level-the better for the world business.

#3.

A smile is the minimum asset balance that you have to maintain on your face-either if you are starting a business or representing the marketing and sales face of your organization that deals with customers.

#4.

Time, Tide & customers do not wait for anybody.

#5

Never argue with customers. It is better to lose an argument & win your customer for life time rather than to win an argument & lose your customer for a life time.

#6

Feedback on your product/service is the biggest gift that a customer can provide you. This feedback is complimentary and worth a billion dollars as it comes from the user. A customer lives with your product and has the most experience – good or bad - about your product. Customers do not have the intent to complain about –until your product performance prompted them.

#7

Design Thinking has to become part & parcel of any organization. As a manufacturer/IT service provider, it becomes mandatory to identify the pain points of customers and provide solutions that are technologically possible and economically viable.

#8

There are three things from an economic and marketing perspective:

Needs, Wants & Must have luxury. With rapid advancements in technology, we have seen how wants becomes needs. Today, "Must have luxury" is the mantra.

As private companies work on R&D, Product development, costing & make otherwise expensive products more affordable for the common man-" Must have luxury" products find way into the hands of the common man and this is the silver line of globalization. An electric car –a "Must have luxury" today will become sooner affordable to the common man. With TESLA & ELON MUSK relentlessly working on cost & subsequent pricing.

#9 - Stepping up Value Chain.

A decade back we saw how manufacturers bought parts from suppliers. Today, the change is that companies like AMAZON are buying the supply chain-the supplier, logistics service providers, ware houses, dealers, distributors. Also to include is the arrangement with banks for loans to customers & Insurance companies to back up claims. Technology has made it possible, thanks to globalization too. The mantra here is to constantly add value by stepping up from parts to sub-assemblies to products.

#10 - The concept of KING

Traditionally it is said customer is the king and this is agreed and remains same as the sole purpose of business is the customer himself.

The new addition that organizations worldwide learned is cash is king. To manage business properly, the need to generate revenue from business done is accepted.

Today with innovation companies & Data Analytics emerging as a high-end tool to enhance business- Anyone who knows how to capture Data continuously, streamline Data, segregate Data, analyze data and use Data for the betterment for the organization & the customer is the KING.

Customer &supplier's/service providers are becoming included in the concept of king- making a positive impact in the lives of people worldwide Qualitatively & Quantitatively. Simply put-selling life style is the order of the day.

CHAPTER 2

Metrics and Importance of Competence

Importance of competitive pricing

Basis of Customer Satisfaction & Metrics

CUSTOMERS COME TO us for the relatively lowest price and stay with us for the highest quality.

Quality by any margin of definition refers to the highest standard.

Customers coming to us for the relatively lowest price does not mean they are looking at a lower price for inferior quality and a higher price for higher quality.

The message is that across the world quality means correlation to the highest standard with no compromises.

Metrics & Importance of competitive pricing

Measure of performance are evaluated with respect to several features and as a common widely accepted criteria following are accepted standards across the globe. Some of the key base aspects that constitute measure of performance are

- OTD (ON-TIME-DELIVERY)
- ACCEPTED QUALITY LEVEL
- RELATIVELY LOW PRICE.
- RESPONSIVENESS
- SAFETY
- ETHICS
- DATA PROTECTION
- AND MANY MORE AS OUTLINED BY THE INDIVIDUAL CUSTOMER.

Metrics & Importance of On-time Delivery

- Importance of -ON-TIME-DELIVERY:
- Delivery to schedule and on a promised date is of primary importance.
- A delay in delivery to start with immediately ends up with a disappointment for customers.
- But more things to follow as reasons for this disappointment
- In the case of B2B, the customer's internal manufacturing schedule is based on the supplier delivery –any delay will off-set and upset his production plan.
- A delay in supplies to the customer will result in production stoppages causing loss of machine hour, man hours resulting in capacity loss.
- Time lost cannot be recovered.
- A loss in machine hours and man hours Cannot be compensated and ultimately lead to increased cost resulting in lowered profits. Other way around –how does it affect the supplier from a financial perspective.
- A delay or a deferred delivery from a supplier side –will immediately postpone the supplier payment receipt from the customer.
- A deferred payment will cripple the cash flow and in extreme cases lead to the non-fulfillment of statutory obligations.
- Statutory obligations like payment of taxes, Electricity bills, payment to employees will be hampered.
- What happens to a supplier in B2B because of a delayed supply to his customer on his cash flow, in consequence, happens to the customer as well for the simple reason unless and until the final product is reached to the end user, the manufacturing company does not get paid and this affects the entire system.
- A delayed supply and far more consequences....
- From a strategic view point .... every supplier has to keep in mind that a customer has a choice to work with multiple suppliers.

- A loss of confidence on a supplier will prompt customer to develop alternate suppliers and this will result in a loss of business prompted by reduced sales...the effect is electric and catastrophic for a supplier.
- A loss in business volume to competition is the immediate but serial problem created because of a delayed supply situation that could have been avoided with proper management.
- Time, Tide & customers do not wait.
- Importance of quality compliance
- Impact of failure to AQL of zero defects:
- AQL is Accepted Quality Level
- The AQL in today's world is zero defects or 100% compliance to quality.
- Even though compliance to six sigma standards is the accepted norm-the relevant question is why produce defects at all?
- Why invest in a process that is not foolproof and not capable of eliminating defects?
- Will a defect of 0.1 % be acceptable for testing a COVID-19 vaccine? The results could be fatal.
- A defect would take customers' confidence away and in the context of global business, a zero-defect promise is necessary to instill confidence in end-user.
- A zero defect process is a global challenge and relentless efforts in terms of time, investment, money is required this is the demand of globalization if globalization is to survive and the very best of products is to reach the customers worldwide, a zero defect process that produces 100% good products is the world order.
- Poor quality simply means zero confidence on the manufacturer
- Poor quality is not more about 99.99% good products but all about .01% defects that results in 100% zero confidence from a customer & end user perspective and by word of mouth this is destructive for business itself, more so for globalization.
- Poor quality is more about the percentage found as defects. Rejection of parts leads to a discussion on rework and scrap. Scrap is a complete loss and rework is an increase in loss and a decrease in profits.
- Rework leads to an exclusive task team for salvage, a specialized method in process, many times specialized machines and dedicated tools, equipment Importantly, the time set apart for rework is more than standard process time –this time is exclusive and very costly for manufacturer.
- Customers & Responsiveness.: Again, the world immemorial &now: Time, Tide & customers do not wait. The customer as an end user is the right person to narrate the product irregularities the way he finds it

on a day-to-day usage. Customer complaints and grievances have to be addressed in the shortest time possible.
- Competition between manufacturers /service providers has to be on time related to responsiveness and this should be restricted to minutes not hours and whichever firm can address grievances in the shortest time shall assume leadership position, the factors like On time delivery, AQL to zero defects, and relatively low pricing being built-in already.

Customers & responsiveness:

- Manufacturers and IT service providers need to remember that every customer is unique and the factor of time is varied from customer to customer but that time is the most irrecoverable asset and loss of time due to a bad product, a product default, a IT bug would be a nightmare for a customer. Your customer can have a bad moment, a bad day, a bitter experience, a night mare but none of them should be because of your product or service.
- The larger the impact of your product on a customer's life style –the chances of your winning lifetime customers are very high.

CHAPTER 3

Customer Satisfaction Index Measurement

- Customer Centricity
- Customer is the King.
- A Satisfied customer is the best advertisement.
- Customers come to us for relatively lowest price & stay with us for quality.
- Importance of smile- you smile and your customer returns the smile-half the problem is addressed.
- It costs 14 times the original cost to bring back a lost customer-makes sense to retain customer.
- If you do not kill your cash cow. Your competition will.

Customer Centricity

- Customers come to us for price and stay with us for quality.
- All through the year 2022 & this year 2023 …how many price reductions have you offered to your customer.?
- Have you ever had your product tested alongside your competition in the eyes of the customer….?

- Has the end user …the car owner/fleet owner ever insisted that the car/truck be fitted with your company product and not your competition… by choice?
- Who is the one individual in your organization responsible to ensure customer satisfaction?
- Who is the one individual in your organization to transform customer satisfaction…to customer delight…Happy customer.?

Basis for Customer Satisfaction Index

- CSI for Manufacturing-
- OTD-ZD(AQL)-Relative Pricing-Zero Accidents.
- CSI for Services-
- OTD-ZD –Responsiveness-IP protection (Fire walls) Relative pricing
- It's always highest quality at the lowest price.
- **Cost reduction is a survival strategy and pricing is a company policy.**

Customer satisfaction

- A work out of customer satisfaction.
- The basis for the customer satisfaction index considered in the following example are ONTIME DELIVERY(OTD), AQL (ACCEPTABLE
- QUALITY LEVEL), and RLP (RELATIVELY LOW PRICING)
- Basis for Customer Satisfaction Index
- CSI for Manufacturing-
- OTD-ZD(AQL)-Relative Pricing-Zero Accidents.
- CSI for Services-
- OTD-ZD –Responsiveness-IP protection (Fire walls) Relative pricing
- It's always highest quality at the lowest price.
- Cost reduction is a survival mechanism and pricing is a policy matter.

Constructing CSI- Manufacturing

- Measuring OTD Compliance.
- Committed schedule based on PO - 5000
- Actual delivered - 4000
- OTD performance – (4000/5000) x 100
- OTD compliance index is…A….

Constructing CSI-QUALITY

- Measuring Quality compliance
- Actual Delivered 4000
- Actual Accepted 3000
- Quality compliance index is (3000/4000) x100
- Quality compliance index is ......B

Constructing CSI-Relative Pricing

- WORKS ON L1, L2, L3...
- L1 IS LOWEST SUPPLIER
- L2 IS SECOND LOWEST SUPPLIER
- L1 gets full 100 points....C
- L2 gets points relative to L1
- Constructing CSI-An example
- Constructing CSI for manufacturing
- OTD 35%
- AQL.....35 %
- PRICING....30%
- Composite CSI is 0.35 X A.+0.35X B+0.30 X C

CHAPTER 4

Transforming Customer Satisfaction to Customer Delight

Cost vs price-customer surplus Cost Reduction is a survival strategy

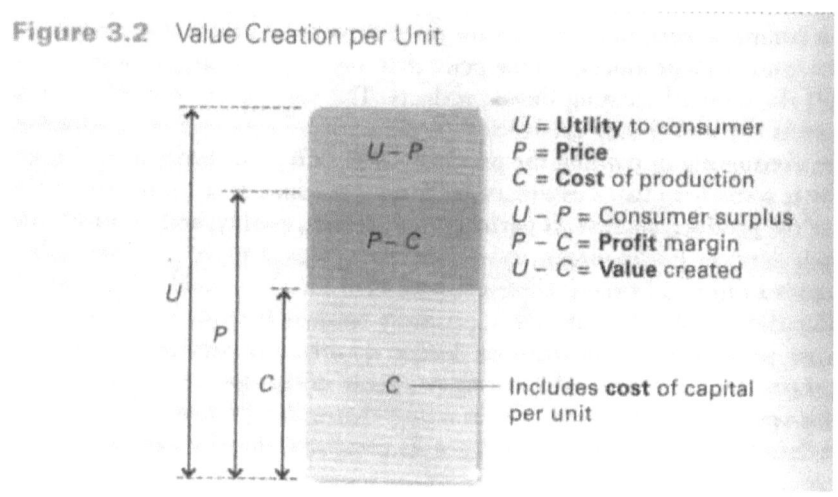

Figure 3.2 Value Creation per Unit

U = **Utility** to consumer
P = **Price**
C = **Cost** of production

$U - P$ = **Consumer surplus**
$P - C$ = **Profit** margin
$U - C$ = **Value** created

Includes **cost** of capital per unit

Cost vs Price-customer surplus: Transforming customer satisfaction to Customer Delight.

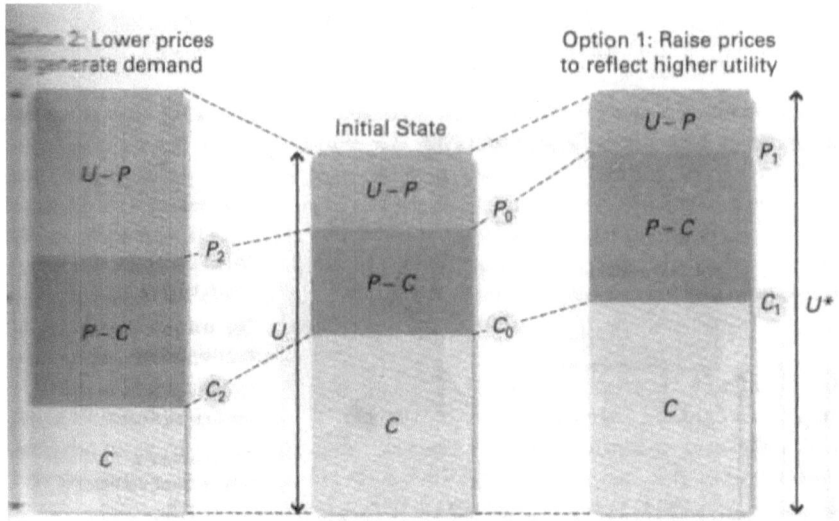

General Motors vs TOYOTA

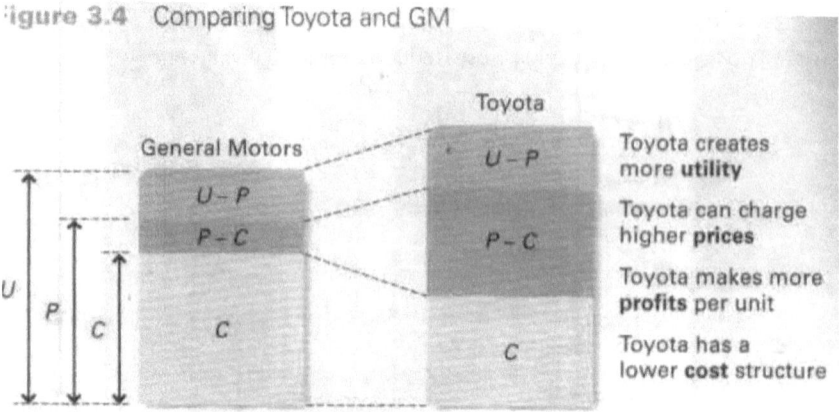

Figure 3.4 Comparing Toyota and GM

Customer surplus

- Customer surplus- simply put is the extra money that the customer is willing to pay for your product over the indicated price.

- This happens purely because of the high positive impact the product has created on his mind, a guaranteed product performance that has itched the name of the brand, the company in his mind.

Importance of high CSI

- A high customer satisfaction index with a high consumer surplus builds goodwill and this is indicated how products by virtue of their performance can help the valuation of the brand and this is a defining moment in a customer–supplier relationship.

Auto Industry-Trends & Strategies

- New product development & changed strategies -
- Challenge-Huge cost of developing new models has risen steeply as a result of design complexity, application of electronics, and new safety and environmental standards.
- In 1980s, cost of producing a new car from drawing board to production line was 1.25 billion. By the 1990s to 2000 the costs had escalated. New car development costs.... during 1990 to 2000.

Ford (1994)/contour	USD 6 Billion
GM 1990 (Saturn)	USD 5 Billion
Honda 1997 (Accord)	USD 0.6 Billion

GM VS FORD

- The biggest learning in the GM–FORD approach is the factor of inclusiveness –listening to your internal employees and taking suggestions, and feedback from them for process & product improvement is a natural, mandatory first step for continuous improvement.
- And that said another definition of the customer is that he is a person who lives with your product –day –in & day out. Your customer knows the good & bad of your product and if you have to have an honest feedback on your product-you should start with your customer.

CUSTOMER DELIGHT

- Transforming customer satisfaction to customer delight-
- The first point is that producers need to be conscious of is price. Need to relentlessly work on cost reduction. Cost reduction is a survival strategy and pricing is a company policy.
- Cost reduction program is synonymous with breathing. Organizations cannot stop working on cost reduction & related cost savings.
- The broad question now is who in the organization is responsible for cost saving? Is it a group or individual? Is it a Function or several departments? is it a base level employee or it at the senior management level…the answer is the answer is: every person in the organization starting from the utility worker at the blue collared level to the top-notch executive- everybody is responsible for cost savings.
- The more cost saved, the more you are in a position to incur higher profits.
- Alongside, you have the option to reduce the price to your customer and this reduced price will provide you an increased market share as for the reduced price you provide to your customer-the customer in turn gives you increased sales
- And this is the simple magic. Customers come to you for relatively low prices & stay with you for high quality. When you are in a position to provide a reduced price, the transformation from being a satisfied customer to a delighted customer has begun. This is just the starting point.
- The customer delight process has begun and there is no end to this. There is a need to constantly keep customers pleased by offering them extra product features, extra after-sales service without additional cost.
- This is the mantra of delighting customers.

Elon Musk & Electric car

- Making the Electric car affordable for the common man.
- Elon Musk…. At some point of time in future…. every car I see in the roads worldwide should be an electric car…realizing dreams…a visionary.

CHAPTER 5

Transforming Customers from Customer Delight to Happy Customer

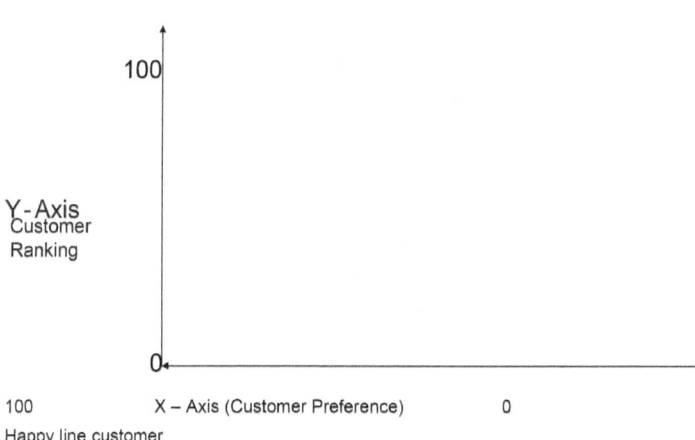

- X Axis-what are key purchasing criteria that matter to customers. /what are customers' preferences between high to low?
- Y-Axis- what is the performance of suppliers' product on the aspects preferred by customers?
- Happy Line, Toyota & customer-centricity

On Happy line & creating Happy customers:

- The construction of the happy line graph is simple.
- On the X-Axis, the plotting of customers most preferred features out of a product is plotted.
- The X-Axis goes from 100 at intersection point and drifts from left to right with zero at the extreme point.
- The Y –Axis is specific to points awarded by customer on aspects preferred by him.
- When this graph is plotted and a curve drawn –the features stand out as below-

Creating happy line graph

- In the features most preferred by the customer on your product, what has been the feature performance as feedback received from customer?
- Are the product ratings on most preferred ratings high and product ratings on least preferred ratings low?
- If this is the case, your product & your company are on alignment with customer requirement.

Understanding Happy line

- If you have a case where the product rating is low on most preferred feature & High on least preferred feature, this means several things are wrong.

1. To start with where does a good performance of a feature of a product come from. The manufacturer has worked hard, has put more focus on Research & development, product development, product testing, field testing, simulation testing on this aspect. There has been a high investment of time, money, methods, practices, machines, tooling's, equipment, training and people and this resulted in the best aspect/feature performance of a product.
2. A high rating on an aspect/feature least preferred by a customer means investment of resources in the wrong areas.
Organizations need to analyze this Happy line customer feedback, Withdraw resources from aspects least preferred and invest in areas on aspects most preferred & having low rating as per customer.

Understanding Happy line graph

When this redeployment of resources happens, there is immediate improvement on these aspects/features that required improvement and this improved product now has a high rating by the customer on aspect most preferred by him.

- A perfect customer-service provider alignment takes place in this happy line customer approach.

Responsibility to create happiness in customers It makes sense to see customers are at Satisfied level by virtue of your product performance.
It takes an effort to transform satisfied customers to delighted customers.
It takes a relentless persuasion to ensure customers are happy – this customer happiness ensures there is alignment between customer & manufacturer and an even more deep alignment of your product with market and this responsibility of an alignment addresses needs of global market.

Constructing Happy line customer

- **Work out Happy Line**

XYZ launched CELL PHONE in June 2022. After a period of 6 months –following are the observations as given below.. OTD is ON TIME DELIVERY, AQL=ACCEPTED QUALITY LEVEL

FEATURE	CUSTOMER PREFERENCE	CUSTOMER RATING
OTD	95 %	60%
AQL (ZERO DEFECTS)	100%	75%
PRICE	90%	70%
WEIGHT	85%	40%
SIZE	70%	35%
STORAGE	75%	50%
BAND WIDTH	80%	40%
Multiple APP compatibility	60%	90%
Elegance	60%	95%
USE BY PURPOSE	60%	60%
After sales service	100%	50%

The first two months' observation was that Demand was unprecedented at 1,00,000 per day and the company failed deliveries. The third and fourth month continued with high demand but added to this there were defects at 20% identified at customer end. The product was priced at Rs 19,100/- plus taxes. In the 6-month period **ABC** Launched T2 5 G at Rs 15,000/-
Construct the HAPPY LINE Graph from customer perspective.
Provide a Business Analyst report based on data and observations provided as above.

- Elon Musk & Electric Car-Must have luxury
- Making the Electric car affordable for the common man.
- Elon Musk.... At some point of time in the future.... every car I see in the roads worldwide should be an electric car...realizing dreams...a visionary.
- Realizing Vision with the mission for the EV car.
- Skimming & Penetrative pricing.
- Mass consumption strategy
- GIGA Concept
- Backward vertical integration.... making electric car affordable for the common man.

Value proposition

- Foremost for the customer
- Second most for the organization.
- Third most for the colleagues & Peers.
- Finally, for myself.
- Align my objective with objective of company
- Who's is responsible for the Profit & Loss of the company?

Value chain initiation

- Kaizen .... continuous improvement.
- KPIs and inclusivity
- One for all & all for one -the organization.
- Sensitivity analysis...if & if Analysis
- 20 % reduction in raw material...
- 10% reduction in WIP
- 10% reduction in FG
- 5% reduction in Non-value added activities
- 3 % reduction in material cost
- 15 % increase in productivity.
- 6% reduction in COPQ. -REJECTIONS & SCRAP
- **BOTTOM LINE.........40% increase in net profits...TOYOTA WAY**

Value chain initiation

- Value chain initiation
- Lean –Eliminating waste
- Far-reaching impacts.
- Six Sigma –capability
- QFD- the ultimate continues improvement in the eyes of the customer- our product against our competition-
- Reducibility, scalability, GAP & sales point.

CHAPTER 6

Customer Centricity & Quality Function Deployment

- Adding prioritized technical descriptors to house of quality

Understanding terms related to customer competitive assessment

- Importance to customer is numerical value provided by QFD team
- Calculation of absolute weight for aluminum=symbolic value x importance to customer
- Calculation of relative weigh of die casting is symbolic value x absolute value
- Target value-a value used to assess whether to keep the product as it is, improve the product or exceed the competition.
- Scale up factor is ratio of target value to product rating.
- Absolute weight=importance to customer x scale up factor x sales point.
- Scale up factor=Target value/product rating
- Sales point tells how well a customer requirement will sell. Objective is to promote the best customer requirement.
- Sales point is a value between 1 and 2 with 2 being the highest and 1 being the lowest.

QFD & Voice of customer

- VOC is the feedback that you get from your customer on your product /service.
- The customer feedback can be in the form of a complaint, grievance, request, demand, issue, poor after-sales service.
- The customer feedback has to be taken seriously and addressed immediately.
- Customer related issues have to be settled to a minimum satisfaction at the earliest.

QFD & Voice of business

- The feedback from the customer is picked up by the marketing & sales department.
- The on-line feedback received from the customer represents the voice of customer.
- The voice of the customer has to be converted into voice of the business.
- And now what does the voices of business mean?
- The voice of business relates to the working of several departments, marketing, sales, Research & Development, product development, production, quality, finance on the customer feedback in conjunction with the customer.
- The outcome of the multi-function departments with the customer deals with gaps to be addressed by the organization taking into consideration the available capability and capacity.
- The Multi-function team works with customer in having the customer rate the product to the feature in comparison with the competition.

QFD & Voice of business

- The resulting mapping of the customer feedback on product improvisation into a matrix is called the interrelationship matrix.
- The biggest advantage of Quality function department is the formation of a multifunction team that works in the eyes of the customer/customer supervised towards continuous improvement.

QFD & VOICE OF BUSINESS

- The advantage of the QFD is that it does away with SILOS-individual departments working in isolation.
- The advantage of QFD is that your product is assessed continuously for performance product features, delivery, quality, after sales service in conjunction with your customer in comparison to your competition.
- Quality function deployment matrix consolidated provides the rating of the customer on your product before execution of a continuous improvement plan and after implementation of continuous improvement and remains a perfect tool.
- The positives after the execution of QFD are:
- Importance to customer-how important is this feature that has been worked for improvisation? The question here is what is the focus to be given on this particular aspect.
- Importance of scale-up factor-The scale up value indicates the amount of effort –in terms of improvisation required to be applied on that area for improvement.
- Scaling up could address aspects like capability, capacity, process & product improvements, relative pricing.

QFD & CUSTOMER CENTRICITY

- Target value-a value used to assess whether to keep the product as it is, improve the product or exceed the competition.

QFD & CUSTOMER CENTRICITY

- The importance of sales point value-sales point is a relative value varying from 1 to 2.
- A sales point value of 2 means that related aspect has highest potential to be sold.
- A sales point value of 1 means relatively this aspect has lesser potential for sales but at the same time important.

QFD & CUSTOMER CENTRICITY

- The term Absolute weight is the guideline in moving forward details the best chances of product improvement taking into consideration a

combination of factors process, process compatibility, cost, investment required, material selection and all.
- Absolute weight indicates the best chances of moving forward for customer satisfaction with a clear continuous improvement plan.

QFD & Understanding terms related to customer competitive assessment

- Importance to customer is numerical value provided by QFD team
- Calculation of absolute weight for aluminum=symbolic value x importance to customer
- Calculation of relative weigh of die casting is symbolic value x absolute value
- Target value-a value used to assess whether to keep the product as it is, improve the product or exceed the competition.
- Scale up factor is ratio of target value to product rating.
- Absolute weight=importance to customer x scale up factor x sales point.
- Scale up factor=Target value/product rating
- Sales point tells how well a customer requirement will sell. Objective is to promote the best customer requirement.
- Sales point is a value between 1 and 2 with 2 being the highest and 1 being the lowest.
- Relative weight =Importance to customer x Absolute weight.
- Customer centricity & Design thinking

CHAPTER 7

Customer Centricity & Design Thinking

- **Design thinking** means keeping the customer in mind all the time while driving innovations which are technologically feasible and economically viable.
- Design Thinking, Tesla & customer centricity

Design thinking - A Car

- Can the car door sense the owner and open by itself...restricted, automated entry?
- Can the car be programmed to allow entry for restricted members of the family...?
- Can the brakes apply themselves on an obstacle been seen...?
- Can the horns sense and blow by themselves...?
- Can ADAS be iterated for high traffic Indian roads....
- Wants/needs to Must –Have luxury...

Design Thinking & CPU- YEAR 1990

If you do not kill your cash cow your competition will...
Challenges with space & business-CPU in 1995

Design Thinking, IBM & Customer centricity-1985-1990

- The challenge
- Initial mode of hardware of CPU was large, weighing in tons and occupying large cubicle spaces. it was cost intensive & highly priced....1990 onwards.
- Business Model- B2B
- Customers –Institutional sales: large business houses, Large educational institutions.

Design Thinking, IBM& customer centricity

- The challenge
- Affordability is a problem-high priced
- Inflation even in decimals is a challenge.
- Dematerialization
- Turn Around Time-Design to product to market
- Lead time is high

Design Thinking, IBM & customer centricity

- The challenge
- Cost of space
- Cost of MRO
- Reliability in a product with large number of parts
- Complex reducibility due to different parts with different materials Design Thinking, IBM& customer centricity
- The large CPU could not be made available to small businesses, small institutes and the common man
- High cost of transportation
- High cost of erection & commissioning
- High cost of MRO
- Limited market potential
- Restricted to use in offices (not homes)

IN 1981 –IBM comes up with small sized CPU. The IBM PC with the desk top monitor & key board –all of them put together weighed 12.3 KG & RAM at 16 KB. With this, for material consumption of 22,000 tons the number of units sold is 2 Million units sold.

In 2011, Dell comes up with laptop that weighed 3.6 KG & memory 4GB.

Impact on business, for 1,200,000 tons of material consumption, approximately 300 Million units are sold.

The further progress is that in 2013, hand held mobile sets light in weight and relatively far less priced compared to laptops and provide capabilities and capacities

On par with lap top, with features comparable were the new scheme of things.

The learning is that products that constituted as cash cows for organizations need to be continuously worked on product design and new variants provided to customers

That provide improved product features that are very much superior qualitatively and also offer benefits in terms of price, styling and usage.

The take away is that if you do not kill your cash cow, your competition will.

CHAPTER 8

Customer Centricity & Stepping Up Value Chains

- Stepping up value chains
- Length of process ....300 meters.
- Turnaround time....... 50 Minutes.
- Cost involved in process...X
- Operators involved in process...60
- Alternate process...technology
- Length of process ... 100 meters
- Turnaround time....25 minutes
- Producing near net shape.

Stepping up the value Chain-Technology to help

- Demonstration of a cost saving made.
- Cost savings of Rs 400/ per part.
- Current price ...Rs 460/- per part. Traditional casting process
- By technologically superior process. Rs 60 per part ..landed price 400 x 6,00,000=Rs cost savings per year on single part at 6,00,000 Annual usages.

Stepping up cost savings-value engineering & value innovation

- **Part to Product.**
- Cost savings through sub –assembly sourcing
- Cost savings equation…stepping up cost savings.
- Other qualitative benefits….
- Selective assembly…Zero rejections…COPQ to near zero. Using capacity for other core –criticalities…

Strategies for Managing suppliers for cost reduction

- Leveraging-Building up economies of scale.
- Stretch-Building up economies of scope.
- Supplier rationalization & 60/40 rule.
- Cost reduction target setting-yearly 10% minimum.
- Working on TAKT time to improve productivity ..to lower cost and relative low pricing.
- Measuring supplier performance through CSI.
- Working out CSI
- CSI= OTD +ZD(AQL)+RLP+Responsivenes+ safety
- Reducing price through shared logistics service providers-ware houses & freight forwarders.

Learning from IT for Manufacturing

Service level attainment	Customer reaction
Below 90%	Inform the media
90–95%	Write to the industry regulator
95–97.5%	Write to the company chairperson
97.5–99%	Contact the complaints department
99–99.75%	It's OK, I suppose …
Above 99.75%	My minimum expectation

CHAPTER 9

Customer Centricity & IT Project Management

IT-Project Management

- The competitive strength of Indian IT –
- Cost Arbitrage (40 to 70%)
- Seamless 24 x 7 working & delivery
- Reach & Spread
- Globally recognized firms
- CMM level 5 certified
- High on ethics and corporate governance
- Scalability
- Depreciating Rupee
- Sustainability for larger customer-service provider relationships
- Bench strength.
- Compliance to Malcolm Baldrige model IT-Metrics-Measure of performance(MOP)
- OTD (on –time Delivery)
- AQL (Acceptable quality levels) Zero Defects
- Relatively low pricing

- Responsiveness
- Data security –Fire wall
- Data Back up
- Safety

Traditional Project Management Tools

PERT is a visual project management technique where we plan, schedule, organize, coordinate and control uncertain activities. Whereas CPM is a statistical technique where we plan, schedule, organize, coordinate and control well-defined activities. CPM is a method used to control cost and time.

- Uncertainty vs certainty.
- Visual technique vs statistical technique.
- Traditional Project Management Tools-CPM & PERT usage
- The Program Evaluation Review Technique (PERT) and the Critical Path Method (CPM) are widely used to manage project circles and activities from conception to the close of the project. The advantage of these quantitative tools is the optimization of project duration, time minimization and project efficiency

CPM vs PERT

- Specific Differences
- CPM is used to control cost and time, and PERT is a must for controlling time when planning.
- PERT is also more of a development and research tool. CPM is more often found in construction project management.
- PERT and CPM also differ in terms of how they estimate.

CPM vs PERT.

- Difference of origin between CPM & PERT
- CPM was designed to improve the scheduling of construction and maintenance activities.
- Was focused on cost, and cost-time tradeoffs.
- Used a single time estimate for each activity.

Original Difference CPM vs PERT

- PERT
- Was designed to co-ordinate efforts of over 3000 suppliers, contractors & governmental agencies in missile project.
- Used three time estimates for each activity-focus was on time.
- Focus was on time-probabilistic completion time & relative cost.

Project crashing

- Project crashing is an extension of CPM and PERT with focus on trade-off between time & cost objective.
- The project crash time is the shortest time that could be achieved if all effort were made to reduce the activity time.

Limitations of GANT Chart

1. GANTT charts do not show the interrelationship among activities which can be large for complex projects.
2. They do not reveal the most limiting path of precedence relationships that should receive the closest attention.
3. A GANTT Chart is most likely happening –it is neither a commitment nor a promise.

CHAPTER 10

Customer Centricity with Agile & Scrum

Agile VS Scrum

- Agile-
- Agile project management (APM) is an iterative approach for planning, guiding projects. It breaks project down into smaller cycles called *sprints.*

Agile

- Agile is a project management tool.
- Agile helps and guides to manage projects better.
- Agile is useful in managing large complex projects.
- Agile methodology is to break large complex projects into small units that can be started and done independently.
- The small units can be delivered continuously and independently.
- By this method, the service provider need not wait until the entire project is completed. There is continuous delivery, once the project is started until completed 100%.
- The project is managed for ensuring on-time delivery.
- Small units are called sprints.

- Compliance to the delivery and quality requirements of each sprint ensures the overall project is well managed.
- Agile & Business model
- Agile is fine-tuned for the Time and material business model.
- The reasoning behind Agile fitting into the Time and material model is that for large complex projects, there is no clarity on the scope of the project to start with or there are continuous changes to scope of project.
- Agile & project management
- As the project proceeds, new requirements are fed into the scope of the project.
- New requirements are in the form of change notes and these change notes can be in the form of a document, SMS, wasp, or email and irrespective of the form it takes, the change asked for has to be incorporated immediately.

Agile & Project Management

- There are two striking points about responsiveness: Immediate Acknowledgement of change request and implementing the change requested at the earliest possible.
- One of the key aspects of Agile is its ability to respond to and factor in changes in scope of project as the project progresses and is finally completed.

Agile VS Scrum

- Agile –process of splitting complex, large projects into small parts and delivering the small parts continuously instead of waiting to complete the entire project to deliver.
- Scrum- Accomplishing twice the work in half the time. Quick wins.
- Continuous improvement is core to both Agile and Scrum conducted in the eyes of the customer- taking continuous customer feedback and improvising process.
- Significance of Agile & Scrum in Indian IT services
- Indian IT firms pay employees on a monthly basis (salary).
- Indian IT firms pay employees and suppliers in Rupees.
- Indian IT firms bill customers on an Hourly basis.
- Indian IT firms invoice customers in USD.
- Commitments are in terms of project hours and either the fixed price model or the T & M model is used.

- Project hours lost will not be compensated and cannot be billed.
- Projects rejected in full mean disappointment to customers and loss to Indian IT service Providers & a loss of business to customers.
- Agile: Initiate& Prompt customer feedback
- Agile focus is to work in small batches, anticipating process changes and collaborating with end users to gain feedback. Continuous releases are a primary focus.

Agile & Responsiveness

THE MAIN BENEFIT of getting started with Agile project management is its ability to respond to issues that arise throughout the course of the project. Making a necessary change to a project at the right time can save resources and help to deliver a successful project on time and within budget.

Agile & Elimination of large scale failure

The Agile methodology enables teams to release segments as they're completed. This continuous release schedule enables teams to demonstrate that these segments are successful and, if not, to fix flaws quickly. The belief is that this helps reduce the chance of large-scale failures because there's continuous improvement throughout the project lifecycle.

Agile & Continuous Evaluation

- In Agile, there is continuous evaluation of time and cost as they move through their work. To name a few Agile uses Azure, velocity, burn down and burnup charts to measure their work to track progress.
- Sprint sessions run from the initial design phase to testing & quality assurance.

The Agile differentiation

- Many organizations use project manager in Agile -- particularly for larger, more complex ones. These organizations have project managers in coordinator role, with the product owner being the prime responsible.

- Agile does not require a project manager –it is not mandatory. Project manager's role under agile is distributed among other team members.

AGILE-Core Values

1. Individuals and their interactions are valued over their processes and tools used.
2. Creating working software is valued over producing comprehensive documents.
3. Customer collaboration is more valued than negotiating contracts.
4. Responsiveness to changes is valued over following a set plan.
5. Five phases of Agile Project Management

There are five main phases involved in the APM process:

Envision.
1. The project, and overall product is conceptualized, needs of the end customers are identified. people who are going to work on this project and stakeholders are in the same team.

- **Speculate.** Team works together to discuss the features of the final product, then identify and set milestones involving the project timeline.
- **Explore.** The project focuses on staying within project constraints, but teams will explore other alternatives also.
- **Adapt.** Delivered results are continuously reviewed and teams adapt as required. This phase focuses on corrections that occur based on customer Feedback. Feedback is constantly given so each unit of the project meets end-user requirements. There is improvement in a project with each iteration.
- **Close.** The final project is measured against updated requirements. Mistakes encountered in the process should be reviewed to avoid similar issues in the future.

AGILE-Concepts, Framework-Impact on International Business

- SILOS-one of the major problems with manufacturing companies is that they have departments /functions working in isolation. The only instance the departments work together is during New product development. The

working in isolation is changing though to working as Multifunctional teams but the transition is slow.
- One major advantage of Agile is that it does away with silos as multifunctional teams are working in conjunction with customers right from the start.

Agile & Time boxing

- Time boxing is about how much time a person will spend on a certain task in a IT project and when you will spend the time.
- In terms of better time management, you block your time in the calendar that you will spend in a certain task in the future.
- Agile Way-Managing offshore projects

Demonstration of Time boxing concept

AGILE-Concepts & Framework-Impact on International Business

- AGILE & TIME BENEFITS. -There is a conscious effort towards business process Alignment & Developing technology systems.
- Large benefits both qualitatively & quantitatively are achieved by both customer & service providers with cost of poor quality to zero
- By focus on software, the Simplicity of software design the project ensures deliver success for both customer & service providers.
- The bottom line is that there is a win –win situation created with the customer able to get the product to the market in time line stipulated.

AGILE-Concepts & Framework-Impact on IB

- SILOS-one of the major problems with manufacturing companies is that they have departments /functions working in isolation. Only instance the departments work together is during New product development. The working in isolation is changing though to working as Multifunctional teams but the transition is slow.
- One major advantage of Agile is that it does away with silos as multifunctional teams are working in conjunction with customer right from the start.

LEAN, AGILE & SCRUM-Impact on IB.

- **Points to ponder**
- Few Project Management tools
- Gantt charts
- PMP as a tool
- CPM
- PERT
- Project Crashing.
- Lean-yellow belt-green belt-black belt-LEAN Master
- Lean vs Agile Vs Scrum

Agile-concepts & methodology Impact on IB.

- Product owner characteristics, responsibilities
- Domain/technical/relative role in manufacturing
- Transparency to the fore-front.
- Mechanism of demand work requirements-gap filling
- Breaking complex large software projects into small incremental projects.
- **Delivering software projects frequently in phases without waiting for Total completion.**
- **Consideration-changing software requirements –reasoning – end user –the customer is the king.**
- Cross functional teams are involved-elimination of SILOS.
- Cross Functional Teams-Planning, Analysis, Design, coding unit testing & acceptance testing.

Agile-Concepts & Methodology-Impact on International Business

- Eliminating a Z category defect. A part with defects that lands in the the hands of customers lead to Fatal implications.
- Rejection of a completed project that does not meet customer requirements is poor performance.
- The cost of Poor quality is to be eliminated.
- The customer-centered approach is built in Agile.
- Agile is a value-driven method.
- V Model- The waterfall model is a plan-driven model. Agile-Projects are driven in the eyes of the customer.

Scrum Introduction-Impact on International Business.

- Scrum exclusive- is software development.
- Sprint-Time boxed iteration:
- Sprint-Break complex projects into small milestones Time-Boxed daily meeting-10-15 -15 rule.
- Meetings and types-sunshine/coffee/stand up/hands-on meeting
- A necessity in international business-scope of project changes-impact on the cost of the project
- HR Wage bill impact.

SCRUM-Product owner

- Scrum-Methodology allows us to get real-time feedback on work and work progress.
- Sprint- The team decides how many work items they can get done in the next 15 days.
- Focus on the velocity of the project.
- The factor of three- Once the project started the team project speed was three times what they were initially.
- Scrum-Belief-Actual product is the important part: Focus on customers and stakeholders.
- Scrum master
- Ensures Focus.
- Identifying and removing impediments.
- Sprint-10:10:15
- Customer requirement change during project is inevitable.
- Sprint types-
- Sprint review & sprint retrospective.

Sprint.

- **Sprint review**:
- How much of project is completed.
- Content completed vs content promised.
- How much can be done in committed time.
- What can be done differently?

sprint

- Sprint retrospective
- What went well so far.
- What did not go well…
- Agree on continuous improvement.
- RCA-Root Cause Analysis-4 W s and 1 How.
- RCA-corrective action & continuous improvement.
- Customer centricity & Azure

CHAPTER 11

Azure & Project Management

Work item process & project Management

1. BASIC
2. AGILE
3. SCRUM
4. CMMI

Objective-Provide access to client to understand

1. progress of project.
2. Handle the people in the project.
3. what portion of work is completed.
4. what portion is to be completed.
5. Factor of time-address.
6. Learning value.

Software Defects in a IT Project

A SOFTWARE DEFECT IS an error, flaw, failure, or fault in a computer program that causes it to produce an incorrect or unexpected result, or to behave in unintended ways.

A software bug occurs when the actual results don't match with the expected results.

Developers and programmers sometimes make mistakes which create bugs called defects. Most bugs come from mistakes that developers or programmer make.

Bug classification

Critical. A core functionality of the system fails or the system doesn't work at all.

Major. The defect impacts basic functionality and the system is unable to function properly.

Moderate. The defect causes the system to generate false, inconsistent, or incomplete results.

Minor. The defect impacts the business but only in very few cases.

Cosmetic. The defect is only related to the interface and appearance of the application.

Examples -ATM Activation & software bug

- Minor Bug-Cash dispensed but no statement.
- Moderate Bug-Cash dispensed but no statement but sms received,
- Major Bug-Cash dispensed statement, sms, email received but cash not dispensed.
- Critical- No response to card.
- why critical- was ATM prompted to fail.

Trouble shooting the Bug-Process

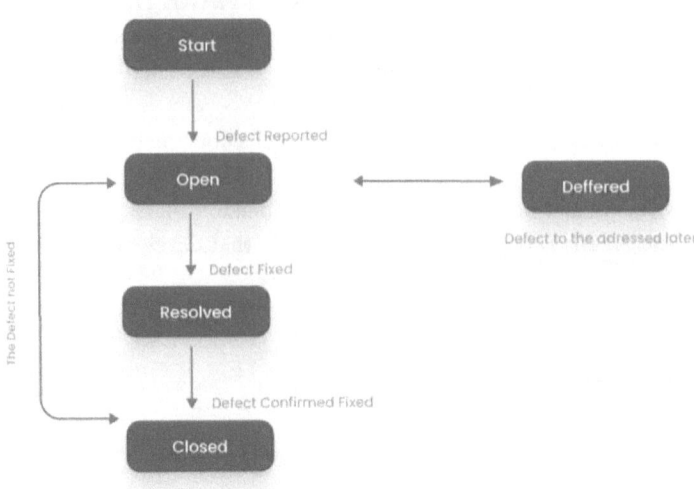

Trouble shooting the Bug-Conclusion

Most defects occur because of the mistakes in program design, source code, or in the operating systems on which the program is running.

While QA experts put constant effort into preventing defects occurring in software programs, software defects in products are still a routine occurrence. For a software system or program to perform its functionality accurately, it needs to be **100% bug-free.**

Agile & Measure of performance

- OTD-Failed delivery, project stoppage, project failure, project deferred
- OTD is on-time delivery
- AQL- 99.9976 % & above
- AQL is an Acceptable Quality Level.
- Responsiveness-minor changes-major changes. ability to understand and immediately implement.
- Data security
- Data backup.
- Relatively low price.
- Shortened project time & customer delight.
- Customer-centricity is the core of Agile & Scrum.

The Multi-Functional Team

- A multifunctional Agile team at a basic level
- STAKEHOLDER
- PROGRAM DEVELOPER
- QUALITY TESTER
- PRODUCT OWNER/SCRUM MASTER
- OPERATIONS EXECUTIVE. (Dev Ops)
- TEAM –LEAD.

Project Management Software

- Project Management software
- There is several project management software, some of the widely used in IT are
- AZURE DEV OPS.
- JIRA
- Trello
- Todoist
- Asana

Agile VS Scrum

- Agile –process of splitting complex, large projects into small parts and delivering the small parts continuously instead of waiting to complete the entire project to deliver.
- Scrum- Accomplishing twice the work in half the time. Quick wins.
- Continuous improvement is core to both Agile and Scrum conducted in the eyes of the customer, taking continuous customer feedback and improvising process.

Significance of Agile & Scrum in IT

- This discussion is specific to Indian IT Companies & their MNC Customers.
- Indian IT firms pay employees on a monthly basis (salary).
- Indian IT firms pay employees and suppliers in Rupees.
- Indian IT firms bill customers on an Hourly basis.
- Indian IT firms invoice customers in USD.

- Commitments are in terms of project hours and either fixed price model or T & M model is used.
- Project hours lost will not be compensated and cannot be billed.
- Projects rejected in full mean disappointment to customers and loss to Indian IT service Provider.

Agile-concepts & Methodology Impact on IB.

- Product owner characteristics, responsibilities
- Domain / technical / relative role in manufacturing
- Transparency to the fore-front.
- Mechanism of demand work requirements-gap filling
- Breaking complex large software projects into small incremental projects.
- **Delivering software projects frequently in phases without waiting for Total completion.**
- Cross functional teams (CFT)are involved-elimination of SILOS.
- CFT-Planning, Analysis, Design, coding, unit testing, and acceptance testing.
- Agile-Concepts &methodology-Impact on IB
- Eliminating a Z category defect. A part with defects that lands in the Hands of customer-can lead to Fatal implications.
- Reject a completed project that does not meet customer requirement. Avoidance of COPQ.
- Customer centered approach.
- Agile is a value driven method.
- V Model- Water fall model is a plan driven model.
- Agile-Projects driven in eyes of the customer.

Scrum-Impact on International Business

- Scrum exclusive-SW development.
- Sprint-Time boxed iteration-
- Sprint-Break complex projects into small mile stones Time-Boxed daily meeting
- 10-15 -15 rule.
- Meetings and types-sunshine/coffee/stand up/hands-on meeting
- Necessity in international business-scope of project changes-impact on cost of project
- HR Wage bill impact.

Scrum Introduction-Impact on IB.

- Scrum exclusive-SW development.
- Sprint-Time boxed iteration-
- Sprint-Break complex projects into small mile stones Time-Boxed daily meeting
- 10-15 -15 rule.
- Meetings and types-sunshine/coffee/stand up/hands-on meeting
- Necessity in international business-scope of project changes-impact on cost of project
- HR Wage bill impact.

SCRUM-Product owner-IB impact

- Scrum-Methodology allows to get real-time feedback on work & work progress.
- Sprint- The team decides how much work items they can get done in next 15 days.
- Focus on velocity of project.
- Factor of three-Once the project started the team project speed is three times than what they were initially.
- Scrum-Belief-Actual product is the important part:
- customers & stake holders.
- Scrum master
- Ensures Focus.
- Identifying and removing impediments.
- Sprint-10:10:15
- Customer requirement change during project is inevitable.
- Sprint types-
- Sprint review & sprint retrospective.

Sprint.

- Sprint review:
- How much of project is completed.
- Content completed vs content promised.
- How much can be done in committed time.
- What can be done differently?

Sprint

- Sprint retrospective:
- What went well so far.
- What did not go well…
- Agree on continuous improvement.
- RCA-Root Cause Analysis-4 W s and 1 How.
- RCA-corrective action & continuous improvement.
- Azure
- Work item nomenclature
- Basic
- Agile
- Scrum
- CMMI
- Work item is related to project management
- How to steer the project focus?

Azure & Work Item

- Under work- item: the objective is how to split up work and do.
- Work item is used for the distribution of work.
- Under the work- item, tasks are to be set up.

Azure

- Version control
- Development and testing procedure
- Version control focus is on development.
- Scope changes, corrective actions, and iterations form part of version control.
- Project Management-Off shore IT development services

How do you manage offshore software development?

- **Best Practices for Managing Dedicated Offshore Teams** Define a Strategic Vision. ...
- Set a Clear Product Roadmap. ...
- Develop a Proper Communication Strategy for an Offshore Team. ...
- Employ Agile Approaches. ...
- Operate with Overlap Work Schedule. ...

- Effective Onboarding and Knowledge Transfer. ...
- Avoid putting overwhelming requirements.

IT development services

Offshore development means outsourcing the software project to a company that is based in another country. For instance, if your company is based in the US, any company that is a part of the United States is considered as onshore.

IT development services

What is onsite and offshore model? Onsite and offshore model is a mixed type of cooperation within software development projects. A customer collaborates both with in-house IT teams and remote teams. Developers' work is coordinated by dedicated project coordinators or managers.

IT development services

Types of Offshoring

- Production Offshoring – This is when a company offshores its manufacturing unit, importing the finished products from the offshore location to sell in the domestic market. ...
- Services Offshoring – This is when a company sets up units in other countries to perform service-related operations.
- IT development services

What studies are required for an offshore project to proceed?

- Feasibility studies phase.
- Conceptual design phase.
- Front-end engineering and design (FEED) phase.
- Construction phase.
- Operation and maintenance phase.
- Decommissioning phase (if applicable)

IT development services

Agile & project management

- The first monitoring plot made available is the plot between earned value on Y –axis and project progress on x axis. The curve trajectories of estimate & actual are compared with real data captured automatically converted into visual graphical mode & made ready for project review & analysis.
- This process covers the complete project including all small teams and monitored day-in and day out continuously for ensuring delivery on –time.

BCWS & BCWP

- Introducing BCWS & BCWP
- BCWS-Budgeted cost of work scheduled
- BCWS-Target set.
- BCWP-Budgeted cost of work performed.
- BCWP=Estimate x percentage completed.

Agile & Time boxing

Project	Hours EST.	Hours ACT.	% Completed	BCWP
Time Box 1(week1)	50			50
Task 1	20	20	100	20
Task 2	30	25	100	30(50)
Time Box 2(week 2)	60			
Task 3	40	40	100	40
Task 4	20		100	20(60)

Agile & Project Management

- A plot of BCWS & BCWP
- BCWS is budgeted cost of work scheduled.
- BCWP is the budgeted cost of work performed
- The plot gives a clear idea of performance on cost angle.

Agile & Project Progress

TIME BOX	BCWS	BCWP
Time box 1	50	50
Time box 2	60	60

BCWS & BCWP

- BCWS-Budgeted cost of work scheduled
- BCWS-Target set.
- BCWP-Budgeted cost of work performed.
- BCWP=Estimate x percentage completed.
- Project Management-Off shore IT development services

Automated testing tools

- Speedy verification and testing of work is required. It becomes necessary to use less expensive tools.
- Few Automated testing tools are
- NUNIT
- JUNIT
- Test Driven
- Zane Bug.

Attrition & IT project management

- One of the major problem in IT services is executives quitting jobs and joining elsewhere.
- The point to be noted is that any employee in project does off-set the project progress.
- The additional point is that employees have varying levels of skill set based on which they are termed as high, low and medium performers.

Attrition & IT project management

- An illustrative example-
- An IT service provider has 200 people working in a IT project and each gets paid Rs 1,00,000/-and turnover is at 10%. The replacement cost at rule of thumb is 90% of salary and this number is on the conservative side.

Attrition & IT project management

- The cost of Attrition is total employees in project x Attrition rate x Annual salary x 80%
- 200 IT staff at attrition 10% means 20 people quit and are replaced each year.
- A Replacement cost of 80% of a salary of Rs 1,00,000 means cost of each replacement is 80% x 80,000 =16,00,000 a year and this is exorbitant.

Attrition & IT project management

- There are three factors under consideration.
- PA =Performance Assessment score.
- PA score is an assigned value, provided by HR.
- WF=Weighting factor=Assigned value, provided by HR based on attrition trend.
- NWL=Number who left=relates to high performers who left.
- Total score =PA X WF X NWL
- TP=TOP PERFORMER
- AP=AVERAGE PERFORMER
- LP=LOW PERFORMER

Project Management –Off shore IT development services

- calculate Top Performance Total score
- 2.-calculate Middle Performance Total score
- 3-calculate Bottom Performance Total score
- 4-calculate Total score.

Project Management –Off shore IT development services

- Scenario I: No Top performer left but one Average performer and three low performers left.
- Workout approach-
- Assigned performance assessment score:100=AP
- Assigned weighting factor:1.5=WF
- High performers left:0=NWL
- Top performance total score=APXWFXNWL
- 100 x 1.5 x 0=0
- Top performer total score=0
- Learning –It is only the High performers leaving jobs that have an impact on Total performance.

Project Management –Off shore IT development services

- Scenario 2: One Top performer left, two average performers left and no low performer left.
- Performance Assessment score assigned=80=PA
- Weighting factor =1 (Assigned)=WF
- NWL=1 (One Top performer left) =Number who left.
- Average performer score =PA X WF X NWL
- Total Average performer score =80x1x1=80

Project Management –Off shore IT development services

- Scenario 3-
- Three top performers left.
- Performance assessment score=60 (Assigned)=PA
- Weighting factor =0.5=WF
- NWL=3 (as three top performers left)
- Total Low performer score =3 x 60 x 0.5=90

- Learning value –losing of a Top performer is several times worse than losing a medium performer or low performer.
- At a basic understanding level- losing a high performer is 10 times worse than losing a low performer.
- Skill set excellence of IT employees is a defining factor. 183

Project Management-off shore IT development services

- Conclusion –A high score is not desired.
- Related questions are:
- How much is the score deviating from industry standards?
- What are the mechanisms in place to address attrition?

Project Management-IT offshore development services

Agile Manifesto

- Satisfy customers through early
- Welcome changing requirements even late during developments.
- Delivering software to shorter time scale.

USE of Azure

- Purely for project management supervision
- Work item Process-Basic-Agile-scrum-CMMI
- Version Control-Development and testing purpose.
- Focus of using AZURE is to how to steer the project.

IT Project goes Multinational

- Agile project
- Across countries
- Across Diverse cultures.

IT project management challenges

- Multiple Currencies are involved
- Depreciation & Appreciation to the US Dollar happens during the course of the project.

CHAPTER 12
Customer Centricity & Market Demands

- Customer centricity as applied to Needs, wants, and Must have luxury.
- In this fast-changing changing world-nothing remains constant.
- The word Luxury is being replaced by the word Must have luxury.
- People as consumers demand that products be made available to them at Affordable prices and this mindset will put pressure on manufacturing companies & IT services to constantly work to reduce prices.
- Design thinking will be put to maximum use and products thought of earlier as made only for the niche segment will be simplified and made available to the common man.
- Mass consumption strategy, Design thinking,
- And Data Analytics will help make a positive impact on the quality of living worldwide.
- Projects are successful because somebody dreamed about making them success & worked hard to make it a success.

www.ingramcontent.com/pod-product-compliance
Lightning Source LLC
Chambersburg PA
CBHW021038180526
45163CB00005B/2187